T O :

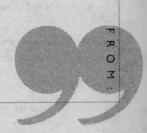

F
R
O
M
:

ZONDERVAN

Love Talk Starters
Copyright © 2004 by Les and Leslie Parrott
Published in association with INJOY, Inc., Duluth, GA

Requests for information should be addressed to:

Zondervan, Grand Rapids, Michigan 49530

ISBN 978-0-310-81047-6

Interior design by Robin Black; UDG Designworks

Printed in the United States of America

09 10 11 12 • 24 23 22 21 20 19 18 17 16 15 14 13 12 11 10 9 8 7

LOVETALK
STARTERS

275 Questions

to get Your Conversations Going

LES AND LESLIE PARROTT

ZONDERVAN.com/
AUTHORTRACKER
follow your favorite authors

PREFACE

A judge was interviewing a woman regarding her pending divorce, and asked, "What are the grounds for this decision?"

She replied, "About four acres and a nice little home in the middle of the property with a stream running by."

"No," he said, "I mean, what is the foundation of this case?"

"It is made of concrete, brick, and mortar," she responded.

"I mean," he continued, "what are your relations like?"

"I have an aunt and uncle living here in town, and my husband's parents are also here."

He said, "Do you have a real grudge?"

"No," she replied, "we have a two-car carport and have never really needed anything else."

"Please," he tried again, "is there any infidelity in your marriage?"

"Yes, both my son and daughter have stereos. We don't necessarily like their music, but the answer to your question is yes."

"Ma'am, does your husband ever beat you up?"

"Yes," she responded, "about twice a week he gets up earlier than I do."

Finally, in frustration, the judge asked, "Lady, why do you want a divorce?"

"Oh, I don't want a divorce," she replied. "I've never wanted a divorce. My husband does. He says he can't communicate with me."

Who could? Let's fact it. Communication requires a few fundamental skills – like accurately listening and understanding what another person is saying. In our book, *Love Talk: Speak Each Other's Language Like You Never Have Before,* we provide a revolutionary method for becoming more understanding and better understood. It's a nononsense method for cracking the code of your most important conversations. But in this little book, *Love Talk Starters,* we set the strategies aside and provide you with 275 literal "starters" to a good talk. Why? Because even after you've acquired all the skills and tools you need for a great conversation, you still need the scintillating content for which they were designed.

We can't tell you how many times we've heard a sincere couple say to us something like, "Once we finally find the time to talk with each other, it seems we don't really have that much to say. We go out to dinner, just the two of us, but the conversation never really takes off." Why is that? They want to have a great talk. They want to connect. So why doesn't it happen? Because they're waiting to stumble upon that unknown topic that will energize and enlighten both of them at the same time. They're looking for that subject that will bring them closer together – whether it be lighthearted, revealing, intriguing, creative, or serious. But those captivating topics don't always come our way – not unless we know where to look for them. That's why we put this little book together.

Love Talk Starters is designed to put 275 intriguing and revealing topics right at your fingertips. Literally. You can thumb through this book to find a conversation starter on each page. There's no rhyme or reason to their order, so don't feel compelled to go one page after the next. Scan for something that catches your attention, put it on the table, and see where it takes you. Some of the questions are just for fun (such as, what's your idea of a dream vacation?), some will educate you about your partner's life (such as, what's their favorite childhood book?), and still others will drill down to something more serious (such as, what's a trait in your partner you most admire?).

By the way, you may want to select one each day or do several in a row. That's up to you. But keep this book nearby. It could be kept at your kitchen table, on your night stand, in your car's glove compartment, your briefcase, your purse, or anywhere else you like. Keep this list of Love Talk starters handy for the next time the two of you would like to enjoy a good conversation, and soon you'll be speaking each other's language. Fluently.

Les and Leslie Parrott
Seattle, Washington

What is your idea of a

dream vacation?

Where would you go?

How would you travel

(or would you travel at all)?

How long would you stay?

What would you do

with your days?

If you were

your partner's

publicist,

what would you want

THE MEDIA to know

about him or her?

On what show would you like

to see him or her be a guest?

What was your
favorite book
as a child and *why?*

What does it **reveal** about your personality?

If you had to build A ROOM onto your house or apartment and you had to spend at least

$100,000,

but you were limited to

just that one room,

what kind of room

would you build

and why?

What is the most difficult

challenge

you faced

before you knew

your partner,

and how would

it have been different

facing it together?

What is the most

romantic

movie

you have ever seen?

Why?

What does your choice

reveal about you

and your romantic side?

If your roles as husband and wife were reversed, how would life for you be easier?

If you, as a couple,

could have dinner with

another couple

history,

who would that couple be?

WHY would you

choose them?

If you did not live

in the country you live in now,

what **country** would you most like to live in and why?

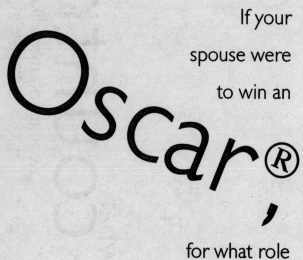

If your
spouse were
to win an

Oscar®,

for what role

would it be?

Which one of you tends
to make more of the

decisions

in your relationship? In other words,
if a scale were used to measure which
one of you tends to hold the final
word, which side would be heavier —
HIS, HERS, OR
WOULD IT BE EQUAL?
How do you feel about this balance?

Over the course of
your marriage,
when do you recall most
deeply
missing
your spouse?

What personal

annoying habit

of your partner's has become

endearing for you over time?

In other words,

name something that

used to BOTHER YOU

that you've now come to

APPRECIATE because it's a

part of who your spouse is.

If you could
relive one day in the
life of your marriage,
which day
would it be?

When are you
most likely to feel

deeply
connected
TO YOUR SPOUSE?

This could be

a time of year,

a time of day,

or a day of the week.

It's up to you.

If your marriage were to have a HOME PAGE on the Internet, how would it look? What would it say?

How does

your spouse help you

restore your

energy?

Be specific.

What one area
OF YOUR MARRIAGE
would you most like

to improve

over the next year,

and how can you do so?

How does each of you bring *humor* into your marriage? Be *specific*.

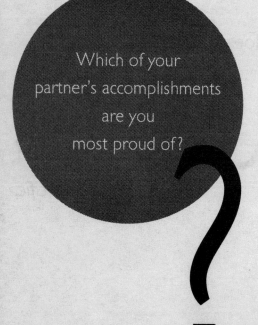

Which of your
partner's accomplishments
are you
most proud of?

If your spouse were a **professor** *of marriage,* which of his or her "LECTURES" would be most popular?

What was

your *favorite*

childhood Christmas

gift?

What is the
most tender way
your partner says **"I love you"**

..without using words?

What

memento

in your home

represents a favorite

marriage memory?

How do you

most like to be

GREETED

by your spouse

at the end of the day?

What one quality
of your spouse
would you most like
to emulate?

In what way are you
and your partner's

personalities

most alike, and how

does that contribute

to your relationship?

What quality do you most

admire

about your IN-LAWS?

What was the
most helpful piece of
advice or WARNING you have ever received? WHY?

What was the

least helpful

piece of ADVICE,

or WARNING,

you have ever received?

Why?

The famous love POEM found in 1 Corinthians 13 depicts several qualities of

love

(patience, kindness, not self-seeking, not easily angered, always hopes, and so on).

Which quality are you THE BEST at?

Which quality do you *NEED TO PRACTICE* more?

What word of

advice

would you give

to a couple

about to be married?

Which of
your wedding gifts
that you still have is
most meaningful
to you?

What is the most

embarrassing

MOMENT you have

shared as a couple?

What do you miss most about your **dating days** together, and how can you bring that into your **marriage?**

What is one of your favorite

romantic songs?

What does your choice reveal about you?

What **compliment** do you most like to hear from your PARTNER? *When did you last hear it?*

conversation
conversation
conversation
conversation
conversation
conversation

What is one of your

favorite topics of

conversation

with your spouse?

conversation
conversation
conversation
conversation
conversation
conversation

When do you
feel most celebrated
by your partner?

What would you like

your marriage

to be like

in ten years?

When it comes to

decision making,

which one of you

tends to be

MORE CAUTIOUS?

Why?

What is the most

relaxing

thing you do

with your partner?

What is your
favorite AUTUMN
tradition?

How has your partner

helped you

become the person

you want to be?

What aspect
of your marriage
are you often
thankful for?

How does

YOUR MARRIAGE

draw you

closer

to God?

How does
the house
you grew up in
compare
to your partner's?

If you had

one hour a day

of UNINTERRUPTED

time

to share

with your partner,

how would you spend it?

What one thing

could you personally do

to improve

communication

between you

and your spouse?

What does
your partner do
that builds your trust
in him or her?

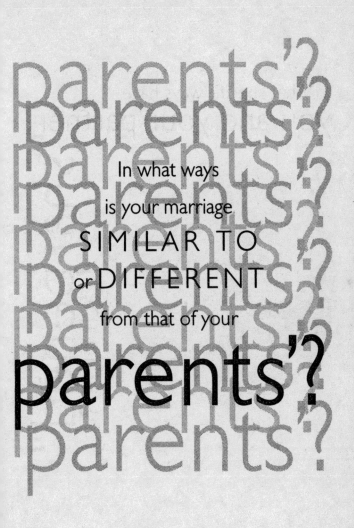

In what ways
is your marriage
SIMILAR TO
or DIFFERENT
from that of your

parents'?

In what specific ways have
you and your partner "sharpened" each other?

What patterns of behavior —

for better or worse —

did you establish

in your FIRST YEAR

of marriage?

What helps you to

cool off

in the

midst of conflict?

If the PHONE rang

and it was

God

on the line,

just calling to check in,

WHAT would you say

and WHY?

What dream or goal
do you hope to achieve as
a couple before
your 50th wedding
anniversary?

LES & LESLIE PARROTT

When your partner is ill,

how would you rate your

"bedside manner"?

From your

SPOUSE'S PERSPECTIVE,

what would improve it?

celebration
celebration
celebration
celebration

What is your idea

of a PERFECT

wedding-anniversary

celebration?

What is a RECENT EXAMPLE
of how each of you has

compromised

on an issue

and therefore made your marriage less stressful?

What would be the perfect way for

your partner to `wake

you up

in the morning?

How would you

describe your

grandparents'
marriages

to your SPOUSE?

When and where

do you most like

to receive a TENDER

touch

from your partner?

What experience from your

honeymoon

is the most

meaningful or memorable

to you?

What would

the two of you

do with a free Saturday and

$1,000

that had to be

SPENT THAT DAY?

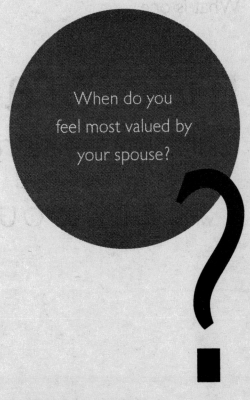

When do you
feel most valued by
your spouse?

What is one

of the most

memorable

Christmas celebrations

you have shared

with YOUR SPOUSE?

What childhood **experience** of yours would be **new information** to your spouse?

On a scale of

1 to 10,

how likely

are you to

give your partner

the BENEFIT

of the doubt?

In specific terms, what **benefits** are you RECEIVING from your marriage that you would not have received *if you had remained single?*

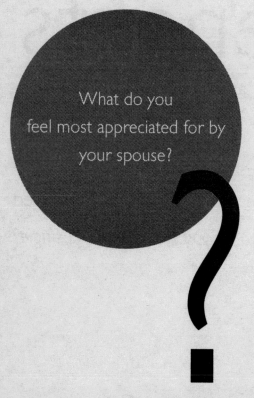

What do you
feel most appreciated for by
your spouse?

If you were the

President and First Lady

of the UNITED STATES,

how do you think it would

specifically impact your marriage?

Why?

Would you like

to have this position

or not?

What does
your spouse do
that makes you feel most

calmed
and
loved?

What do you do that
demonstrates
your LOVE and

APPRECIATION

toward your spouse?

Of the two of you,

which is more accepting of

change

in your lives?

WHY?

Give a specific example.

If you lost your

sight or
your hearing,

how would it **affect** your marriage?

What is a specific way you

support

your spouse?

(In other words,

how do you show RESPECT,

provide a sense of SECURITY,

ENCOURAGE,

COMFORT,

or show ACCEPTANCE?)

What is your number-one

emotional
need *right now,*

and how can

your SPOUSE meet it?

Name a time
when YOU made a

mistake

and your spouse was

full of GRACE,

expressing no criticism.

Name a time when

the roles were REVERSED.

What expression
of affection from your spouse
makes you feel most
deeply loved and
understood?

What **fear** do you have that you have NEVER TOLD your partner about?

What is your

top priority

for this next week,

and how can your spouse

help you accomplish it?

On a scale of 1 to 10,

how would YOU FEEL

to receive a brief call

from your spouse, *just to say*

"I love you"?

How do each

of your ratings differ?

If you were both players on a professional **baseball team,** what positions would each of you play?

Why?

How does this tie into your RELATIONSHIP?

Which topic of conversation do you **most fear** discussing with your partner?

What are some ways
you may have

hurt

your SPOUSE
in the past week?

Are you willing
to apologize?

Imagine

that you are

a WAITER at a restaurant

who made a mistake

while serving you and your spouse.

How would you as the waiter

DESCRIBE THE COUPLE

you were serving?

What impressions would you

have of their marriage?

In what little ways
may you have
neglected
YOUR PARTNER'S NEED
for attention?

*(For example,
in giving respect,
security, or
encouragement.)*

If you could show a

brief video clip

from your CHILDHOOD

to your spouse

depicting any incident

between you and your dad

(mom, schoolteacher),

WHAT would it be

and WHY?

If you were to be

remembered for a piece of

artwork,

WHAT would it be about,

and WHERE

would it be displayed?

What would the perfect

sexually intimate

encounter between

you and your spouse include?

From your perspective,
what would PRECEDE it,
who would INITIATE it,
WHERE would it take place,
what would you be WEARING,
and so on?

What analogy
or word picture
would you use
to describe marriage
to a child?

How has your

FATHER (MOTHER)

roles

as husband and wife?

shaped your

If one of you
is MORE of a

"neat freak"

than the other,
how would you feel

if the roles
were REVERSED?

If you were a pastor

and were going to

preach

a sermon on marriage,

what specifically

would your TOPIC be?

How did

your mom and dad handle

conflict,

and how

has their model

impacted your ability

to resolve conflict

in your own marriage?

What question
would you like to ask
your spouse that
you have
never asked?

Think of a time

. when your mom or dad

apologized

to the other.

What have you
LEARNED about apologizing

to your spouse from

your family of origin?

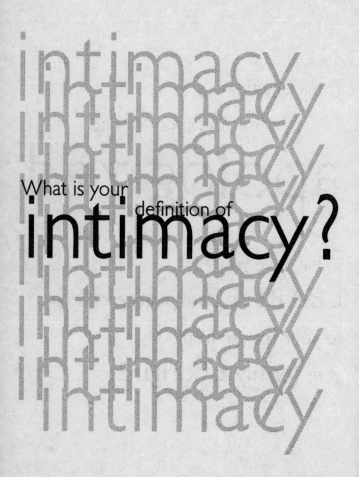

What is your
definition of
intimacy?

Do you as a couple fit the

stereotype

of the husband

rarely asking for directions

when lost?

WHY or
WHY NOT?

What important

life lesson

have you learned

from your spouse?

What causes predictable

stress

in your

marriage?

How was affection

in the form of

physical touch

and

verbal expression

expressed to you

by your mom and dad?

One of the most popular HYMNS of all time is

"Amazing Grace."

Can you identify a specific time when you RECEIVED grace from your partner?

What made it so amazing?

What was your very

first date

like, and W H O

was it with?

How would your marriage be

different

if you had each

been raised by the

OPPOSITE SET

of parents?

What is the
most unselfish thing
that your spouse
has ever done
for you?

What is your

partner's favorite

color?

(It's a pretty basic question,

but most people don't know.

DO YOU?)

How would you

finish this sentence:

"My spouse is

gifted

at..."?

If you were able to

eavesdrop

on another COUPLE

as they toured your home,

what kind of comments

do you think they would make —

not just about your house,

but also about

you and your family?

Which of you is the most
patient person?

think

Why do you think this is so?

What act of

kindness

have you recently ENJOYED

from your spouse

and not

thanked him or her for?

John Milton said

that marriage is

"a heaven
on earth."

For you personally,

what's the most

HEAVENLY ASPECT

of your relationship

and WHY?

Describe your

ideal meal.

WHERE would it be?

WHAT would you eat?

Would it be

breakfast, lunch,

or dinner?

WHY?

If you were
one of the CAST MEMBERS
of the old

Gilligan's Island

television show,

WHICH character

would you be and WHY?

What do your choices

say about your personality

and how the two of you

RELATE to each other?

What is the
one thing in your life
you have been
most proud of in the past
twelve months?
Why?

What is one thing

you can ALWAYS say or do

laugh

to get a

out of

your partner?

Of the two of you,

who is more

resistant

to change?

WHY?

Give an example.

If money were no object,
how would you like
to celebrate
your next wedding
anniversary?

Considering your CURRENT
financial budget,
how would you
REALISTICALLY
like to celebrate
your next
wedding anniversary?

Matthew Porter, the writer,

said to his wife:

"You do something to me —

something that simply

mystifies me."

What does

your spouse do

TO MYSTIFY YOU?

favorite dessert
favorite dessert
favorite dessert
favorite dessert

Name your partner's
favorite dessert.
Does he or she
AGREE with you?

favorite dessert
favorite dessert
favorite dessert
favorite dessert
favorite dessert
favorite dessert

If a police detective

dusted your spouse for your

fingerprints

in the last 12 hours,

what would he find?

Some say the age of

chivalry

is past, that the spirit
of true ROMANCE is gone.
If outsiders were to
evaluate this observation
in the light of your relationship,
what would they conclude?
WHY?

If God were to give

an "ELEVENTH"

commandment

to you or your partner,

WHAT would it be

and WHY?

If you could have

any SINGER

or MUSICAL GROUP

perform at your spouse's

next birthday party,

who would it be,

and what

song

would you have them sing?

It can sometimes be a

struggle

to find another

couple where all four of you can be

GOOD FRIENDS.

Do you have this kind of relationship,

and if so, what makes it work

for all of you?

If not, what seems to be

the BIGGEST HURDLE

to making this happen?

Outside of
your wedding day photos,
what's your most prized
photograph of the two
of you together
and why?

Shakespeare wrote that

"love comforteth

like sunshine after the rain."

In specific terms,

what are the most

COMFORTING THINGS

your partner does for you?

If there were a competition for

humility

in your relationship,

who would win

and why?

How does each of you respond to

disappointment?

What can

each of you learn

from the other

about how to handle

disappointment better?

What's the
best practical

joke

you have ever heard of?

Would you ever like to play

an ELABORATE practical

joke on your partner?

If so, how do you think

he or she would REACT?

Explain this statement:

"Never scratch a

tiger

with a short stick."

How might it

relate specifically to you

and your partner?

Name your partner's top three

hobbies.

Does he or she **agree** with your answer?

If you had to
go without
one of these items for a day,

which would you choose:

your WATCH,

your CELL PHONE,

access to your E-MAIL?

Why?

What's your partner's favorite flower? (This question is not for ladies only!)

Is your PARTNER
more likely to be
influenced
with FEELINGS
or with FACTS?

Give an example

of how you might use

either of these to

change your partner's mind.

Name a
"recreational goal"
that you are both
working on TOGETHER?

If you don't have one,
what is a recreational goal
that you could set?

If there were a

NEW COUNTRY named

"Marriage,"

and you and

several other couples were

in charge of its governance,

what POSITION in the

government *(security, finance,*

international relations)

would you and your partner

hold and WHY?

How would
you like to
CELEBRATE
your fiftieth wedding

anniversary?

If you had met

your partner in the

sandbox

as TODDLERS,

what would you have said

to each other,

considering your

emerging personalities,

at that stage?

What advice

on avoiding **conflict**

would you give

to another couple?

WHY?

Imagine that

you and your parter were

astronauts

exploring the galaxy together.

If the two of you

were to make an

INCREDIBLE

DISCOVERY together,

how would the headline

of your hometown paper read?

Which one of you
is the most competitive?
Why? Where did that
competitive streak
come from?

What is your spouse's favorite

movie genre:

action/adventure,

romance, horror,

mystery, drama,

or comedy?

If you could

orchestrate

an EXACT GREETING

from your partner

at the end of the workday,

what would it be like?

What is one specific way

in the past month that

the two of you have spent

quality time
together?

If you could

magically retrieve one

memento

from the history

of your relationship

(perhaps a ticket stub

or something else

from your dating years),

what would it be?

WHY?

What is the best

Christmas

present

you have ever received

from your partner?

What made it

the "BEST"?

What is the most

PERSONALLY meaningful

tradition

you have

cultivated as

a couple together?

How would
you describe your
partner's sense
of humor?

LES & LESLIE PARROTT

If the two of you could strap on

jet-propulsion
packs

that could travel

up to 3.0 0 MILES in a day,

how would you use them?

If you only had 24 hours

to use these packs,

where would you go

and what would you do?

When was the last time
the TWO OF YOU
together found something really

funny—

laughing?

so funny you literally
could not stop

Do the two of you share any

financial goals

TOGETHER as a couple?

If not, what one goal

for your money might

you set together?

Simone Signoret once said,
"CHAINS do not hold
a marriage together. It is

threads,

hundreds of tiny threads,
which sew people together
through the years."

What tiny threads

have woven your two spirits

together this week?

What's one way
you have each

educated

each other to be

more knowledgeable about

the opposite sex?

When was the last time

you felt completely

secure

with YOUR SPOUSE?

What contributed to this

feeling of safety?

Which of you tends to be more

aggressive

in solving problems?

WHY?

How do each of you approach

time?

Is one of you

more "URGENT"

about things in general

than the other?

Is one of you more

"LAID BACK"?

Why do you think this is?

What are
your partner's top three
personal strengths?
Why do you list
these particular
things?

Every couple has

regrets

that can

WEIGH

them down.

Is there anything

from your history together

that still keeps you

from LIVING FULLY

in the present?

If so, what can you do

to loosen its grip?

If you were to carry a

small object

in your pocket tomorrow

that would remind you

of your S P O U S E ,

what would it be?

If you could do away

with one household

chore

for the rest of your life –

something you would

NEVER have to do again –

which one would you choose?

What is one piece of

unfinished
business

the two of you have?

It may have to do

with FINANCES,

with IN-LAWS,

or ANYTHING else.

What keeps you

from tying up this loose end?

If asked to identify what makes you a unique couple, what do you think other people would say? Why?

How do you feel about

actually SCHEDULING

passionate

evenings

on your calendar?

Would this help

your love life?

Why or why not?

one-word clues
one-word clues
one-word clues
one-word clues

If you were on
the old Password game show
and you had to give your partner

one-word clues

to get them to say the word

marriage,

what would your clues be?

Just as an automobile needs a

tune-up

every few months,

so does a RELATIONSHIP.

If you were to take

your marriage in to a

"relational mechanic,"

what would his suggestions be?

If your relationship were a weather **forecast,** **predicted** what conditions would be for tomorrow?

Can you think of a

goal

you have for

your SOCIAL LIVES

as a couple?

If not,

what goal could you

set for yourselves

right now?

Which would you say

is more important to you:

winning the

approval

of your spouse,

or having

CONFIDENCE

in his or her

loyalty to you?

Poet E.E. Cummings once said,
"The most WASTED
of all days is the
one without

laughter."

What have the

two of you laughed

about today?

What's the
biggest surprise
you have experienced
in the last year
and why?

If you could wear a

magical

pair of glasses

that allowed you

to read

your partner's MIND

for 60 seconds

in a 24-hour day,

when would you

want to wear them

the most?

As a child,

what was your favorite

THANKSGIVING

tradition

and WHY?

Be specific in your answer.

(For example,

just saying

"eating turkey"

isn't allowed!)

If you were to go

without television

in your house for a week,

who would feel

WITHDRAWAL PAINS

the most and why?

What would be the result

of a TV fast for the two of you?

What would

your spouse say is his or her

"guilty pleasure"

these days?

Which MOVIE TITLE

describes your

sex life

the best:

The Fast and the Furious or

The Mummy Returns?

Maybe it's another title altogether—

if so, what is it and why?

If your marriage

were to be given an

"extreme makeover"

by a team of marriage specialists, what would be the most noticeable **difference** to other people?

What would you

predict

is going to be

your partner's

greatest legacy?

What is one of the most

special
moments

you've ever had

with one of your

PARENTS—

either as an adult

or as a child?

If you had
to choose, would you
rather manage
a gourmet grocery store or
a neighborhood deli?
Why?

What is ONE SPECIFIC area in your life that you would like YOUR PARTNER to NOTICE more? In other words, where could you use a little more

affirmation?

Would the two of you

rather have dinner with

Jay Leno or
David Letterman?

Why?

What experience have you had

that caused you to

pause

and QUESTION

something you firmly believed?

If you can't think of one,

what experience have you had

that affirmed

one of your convictions?

What is one
specific thing
you can do TOMORROW

to make your partner's day

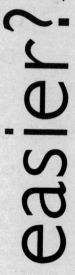

easier?

How do you feel about friendships with the

opposite sex?

Is it possible to be

"JUST FRIENDS"?

Do you think that once

you are married,

specific **boundaries** should be set

around these relationships?

If so, what are

those boundaries?

If you could live

the LIFE

of any one person

in the

Bible,

WHO would it be

and WHY?

What would
your spouse say
is his or her greatest
weakness?

LES & LESLIE PARROTT

When are you

most likely to be the most

selfish

in your marriage?

If your partner were on a

hockey team,

would he or she more likely

be a GOALIE

defending the net

or a FORWARD

on the offensive?

Why?

How does your answer

relate to your relationship?

soul mates
soul mates
soul mates
soul mates
soul mates
soul mates
soul mates

What does it
mean to be
"soul mates"?

soul mates
soul mates
soul mates
soul mates
soul mates
soul mates

In what particular way would you say your spouse is still childlike?

In your opinion,
how are YOU and
YOUR PARTNER

most
alike?

"A PRUDENT QUESTION," asserted Francis Bacon,

"is one-half of wisdom."

In other words,

when we admit we need help,

we become wiser.

In what ways are you

asking questions and

getting help when you need it

as a couple?

If you were a news reporter, how would you describe your PARTNER'S spiritual journey?

What would
you say is your
partner's most beautiful
facial feature
and why?

Recall a time when you felt

affirmed and encouraged

by your partner.

What made this time

so MEANINGFUL

and MEMORABLE?

Recall a time when

humor
"backfired"

in your RELATIONSHIP.

What happened,

and what can you

learn from it?

As a couple,

if you could do

ANYTHING you wanted

as a TEAM and were

guaranteed

NOT TO FAIL,

what would it be?

What is the most helpful

communication
tool

you have used

TO UNDERSTAND

your mate?

If an aspect of your relationship

on any given week

were the equivalent

to walking on a

minefield,

mine

name one

you'd say is probably buried? Why?

Are you influenced more by

facts or by feelings?

WHY?

If you had to choose,

would you be

more interested in

understanding
HISTORY or
predicting
the FUTURE? Why?

On a scale of 1 to 10,

how influenced by the

weather

would you say your spouse is?

In other words,

how much does it impact

his or her mood?

What memory would you like to make together in the next six months?

?

identity change
identity change
identity change
identity change

How did your

identity
change

after you
got married?

Imagine a
continuum
between constantly

BRINGING ATTENTION

to yourself

and desperately trying

TO AVOID IT.

On this continuum,

where do you see your spouse?

Where do you see yourself?

WHY?

Samuel Johnson once wrote,

"I do not call a TREE

generous

that SHEDS ITS FRUIT

at every breeze."

What do you suppose

he meant by that,

and how might it relate

to generosity in marriage?

Can you name a *spiritual goal* you have as a couple? *If not, is there one you can set together right now?*

How would your SPOUSE

respond to this question:

"Describe a time when you felt like you didn't fit in"?

As a child,

were you ever the

victim

of a BULLY?

If so,

what happened?

If you are

like most couples,

you find it difficult to

TALK ABOUT

sex.

Why do you think that is,

and what would make it

EASIER for you?

What was the
first impression
you had of your partner
the first time you
ever met?

Who is the F I R S T person

you would both turn to

when you need

advice?

If you could

trade places

with ANOTHER COUPLE

FOR A DAY just to see

what their life was like,

who would it be

and *why?*

What is your partner's
FAVORITE and
LEAST FAVORITE
season
and *why?*

Complete
this sentence:

"If only I . . ."

If you had to choose between living in the heart of a

big city

or out in the country, WHICH would you choose and WHY?

Some have said that

marriage is not a PROCESS

as much as it is an

achievement.

If you agree,

what kind of a TROPHY

should you two receive

on your next anniversary?

How would the plaque

on it read?

Chances are,

you don't COMPLIMENT each other

as much as you'd like to.

Why is that?

What makes being

affirming

and ENCOURAGING

so difficult at times?

On a scale of
1 to 10, how

polite

are the two of you

to ONE ANOTHER?

If you are not *as polite*

as you'd like to be,

what could you

do DIFFERENTLY?

What would
your partner say you
appreciate the most about
your mother?

What would

your partner say you

APPRECIATE the most

about your

father?

If you ran

one of the major

television
networks,

how would you

CHANGE

its programming?

Answering

BEFORE TRULY LISTENING

is one of the easiest

communication
mistakes

we make in marriage.

Why do you think

this is so?

Do you fall victim

to this error very often?

What SHARED

activities

do the two of you

have that bring you

CLOSER TOGETHER?

If you were to develop

a NEW one,

what would it be?

Have you ever found yourselves

laughing

at something

that NOBODY ELSE

would likely find funny?

What do those moments reveal about your shared humor?

When does your partner

look most

sexy

to you?

If your spouse had a

choice

between a day

at an AMUSEMENT PARK

or a day at a HEALTH SPA,

which would he or she choose?

How about you?

How did

your PARENTS express

verbal affection

toward YOU or

toward EACH OTHER?

How has that IMPACTED

your expression of affection

in your relationship?

Finish
this sentence:
"I like to
be kissed…"

If you could

make your marriage

10%
better

in ONE SPECIFIC AREA

over the next 12 months,

what would that

area be?

Have the
TWO OF YOU
ever considered writing a

mission statement

for your marriage?

What might

it include?

How do you

RATE YOURSELF as a

goal setter?

How do you feel

about setting goals

as a couple?

Can you

name any goals

the two of you have

right now?

Complete this sentence:

"The purpose of our marriage is…"

What are three of the top

highlights

from your

past year together?

Why did you

select these three?

How do the two of you

preserve your

memories

TOGETHER

(a journal, photos, on video, etc.)?

How often do you

REMINISCE about them —

as much as you like

or not enough?

What does such reminiscing

do for your relationship?

If you could change

one thing about

your recent

sex life,

what would it be?

Research shows that

MARRIED COUPLES do

better financially

THAN SINGLES.

Do you think that's

TRUE for you?

Are you better off financially

in your relationship

than you would be

as a single person?

Why *or* why not?

It's not unusual
to feel lonely,
even in your own marriage.
Can you recall a time
when you felt

lonely

recently?

How can your partner

help you feel less alone?

When it comes to

anger,

do you have

a *SHORT* or

a *LONG* FUSE?

Why do you

think that is?

What has
been on your mind
most today?

LES & LESLIE PARROTT

William Shakespeare

once said,

"I WILL

praise

ANY MAN

THAT WILL PRAISE ME."

Do you ever feel this way?

When are you

most willing to praise

your spouse without

an ulterior motive?

Are you aware

of a time that your

partner OVERLOOKED something

annoying

that you do?

WHAT was it?

Have you thanked him or her for their patience?

What are you doing,

or what have you recently done,

to HELP YOUR PARTNER

become a

better
person?

Recall a conversation that you and your partner had recently that was *meaningful* to you.

What made it meaningful?

It's impossible

for MARRIED COUPLES

not to cause each other a little

emotional pain

now and then.

What do you do with your pain?

Do you tend to nurse it or let it go?

Does it depend on

the kind of pain it is?

What makes the difference?

It's so easy sometimes

to find

fault

and lay

blame.

What can you do,

in practical terms,

to AVOID this

easy temptation

in your own marriage?

If all that your

single friends

knew about MARRIAGE

was what *THEY SAW*

in YOUR relationship,

what would they have

to say about it?

Be specific.

Most of us idealize great

love
stories,

partly because we envision

only the most ROMANTIC moments

(especially when it comes to movies).

WHY *do you think we do this,*

and what kind of

POTENTIAL HARM

might this cause

to your own marriage?

LES & LESLIE PARROTT

If you are
crying about something,
how do you typically
want your partner
to respond?

In general,

how do you feel

about professional

counseling?

Is this something you would ever
consider if you needed help?
WHY or WHY NOT?

Trusting

in God can seem pretty

ABSTRACT at times.

Can you think of a time

when the two of you did this

in very realistic terms?

What did that mean

to each of you?

Describe a typical

dinner scene

in the HOME

in which you grew up.

What was

the conversation like?

Do you ever feel like a volcano, building steam and ready to erupt with ANGER and FRUSTRATION? *If so, what do you expect that to accomplish for you?*

Think of a time

when you were being

a bit more hard

on your partner

than you needed to be.

What was the result

and was it worth it?

What interferes most

with the two of you spending

quality
time

together?

What can you

do about it?

What can you remember about your wedding vows? How much of it can you repeat from memory?

Are you ever

tempted

to talk about

YOUR SPOUSE

behind his or her back?

Of course, this is

NOT TYPICALLY A GOOD IDEA.

If it's a temptation,

how do you keep

from doing it?

Humorist FRANKLIN ADAM

was known for saying,

"Too much truth is

uncouth."

Do you see any relevance

for this statement

in your

marriage relationship?

Can there ever be **too much truth** in marriage?

Most marriages

have repetitive squabbles –

irritations

that occur *again and again.*

What are yours?

What can you do the next time

one of them arises to

FOCUS *on a solution*

rather than

DWELL *on the problem?*

Have you ever

caught yourself trying to

deceive

your partner by playing the

"I-WAS-ONLY-JOKING" card?

If so, what was the result?

How do you feel

when you're on the

RECEIVING END

of this tactic?

When it comes
to your spirituality,
how does

doubt

factor into your
FAITH?

Is it good or bad?

Does it DEPEND on something?

If so, WHAT?

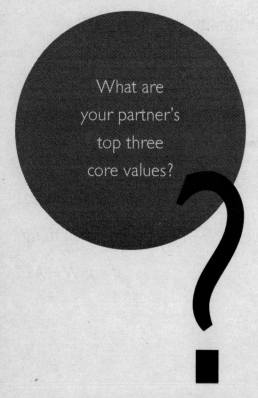

What are
your partner's
top three
core values?

LES & LESLIE PARROTT

Name two

SPECIFIC WAYS

YOUR SPOUSE has made you a

better
person

in the past

12 MONTHS.

Complete this sentence:

"When it comes
to our MARRIAGE,
I love..."

Proverbs 24:26

equates an honest answer

to a KISS *on the lips.*

In what specific ways is

honesty

a ROMANTIC gift

or gesture to you

in your relationship?

CARL JUNG once said,
"The meeting of two personalities is
like the contact of two

chemical

substances: If there is
any REACTION,
both are transformed."

In what specific ways

has your partner transformed you

for the better?

Who took you to school on the first day of school? What was it like for you?

Generally speaking,

on a scale of 1 to 10,

HOW EASY IS IT

for you to

take responsibility

when you are

at fault?

What part of your

wedding
day

do you

remember

and appreciate

the most?

How would you describe your partner's decision making style (spontaneous, cautious or somewhere in the middle) and why?

If there was a

NATIONAL MARRIAGE DAY

each month where

husbands and wives

were required to spend it

doing something that

enriches

THEIR MARRIAGE,

what would you do

with your day this month?

What is it that your partner
says or does
that makes you feel most

respected,
appreciated
and
valued?

What's the most

sentimental
object

you have

from an experience

the two of you share

and *what makes it so?*

Love Talk:

A breakthrough discovery in communication for transforming love relationships.

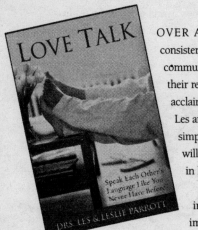

OVER AND OVER couples consistently name "improved communication" as the greatest need in their relationships. *Love Talk*—by acclaimed relationship experts Drs. Les and Leslie Parrott—is a deep yet simple plan full of new insights that will revolutionize communication in love relationships.

The first steps to improving this single most important factor in any marriage or love relationship are to identify your fear factors and determine your personal communication styles, and then learn how the two of you can best interact. In this no-nonsense book, "psychobabble" is translated into easy-to-understand language that clearly teaches you what you need to do—and not do—for speaking each other's language like you never have before.

Love Talk includes:

• The Love Talk Indicator, a free personalized online assessment (a $14.95 value) to help you determine your unique talk style

• The Secret to Emotional Connection

- Charts and sample conversations
- The most important conversation you'll ever have
- A short course on Communication 101
- Appendix on Practical Help for the "Silent Partner"

Two softcover "his and hers" workbooks are full of lively exercises and enlightening self-tests that help couples apply what they are learning about communication directly to their relationships.

LOVE TALK INDICATOR:

The Love Talk Indicator is an online assessment that will help you determine your *Love Talk* style. When you take the assessment you will learn the unique communication style of you and your partner and discover the keys to communicating with each other. The *Love Talk* Indicator assessment is found at www.RealRelationships.com

ZONDERVAN Groupware™:

In this six-session ZondervanGroupware™ video curriculum,

acclaimed relationship experts and real-life couple Les and Leslie

Parrott are back with a wonderfully insightful guide for improving

the single most important factor in any marriage or love

relationship—communication! In Love Talk, *the Parrotts help*

participants discover their communication style, their partner's, and

how the two can best interact. In this no-nonsense curriculum,

"psychobabble" is translated into easy-to-understand language that

clearly teaches partners what they need to do—

and not do—for healthy communication. Learn how to take your

conversations to a deeper level and engage in the most important

conversation you and your partner will ever have. Follow the deep

and simple plan prescribed in Love Talk *and begin communicating*

your way into a happier, healthier,

and stronger relationship.

The six sessions include:

1. Communication 101
2. The Foundation of Every Great Conversation
3. Your Personal Talk Style
4. The Secret to Emotional Connection
5. When Not to Talk
6. The Most Important Conversation You'll Ever Have

The ZondervanGroupware™ edition of Love Talk is
available in curriculum kit that includes a men's workbook,
women's workbook, a DVD, a copy of the book Love Talk,
and a CD-ROM with promotional materials. The DVD is also
available separately as the ZondervanGroupware™ Love Talk
Small Group Edition.

Kit:	0-310-26466-9
DVD:	0-310-26467-7
Booklet:	0-310-26468-5
CD-ROM:	0-310-26469-3
Men's Workbook:	0-310-26212-7
Women's Workbook:	0-310-26213-5
Hardcover Book:	0-310-24596-6

ABOUT THE AUTHORS

DRS. LES AND LESLIE PARROTT are co-directors of the Center for Relationship Development at Seattle Pacific University (SPU), a groundbreaking program dedicated to teaching the basics of good relationships. Les Parrott is a professor of clinical psychology at SPU, and Leslie is a marriage and family therapist at SPU. The Parrotts are authors of the Gold Medallion Award-winning *Saving Your Marriage Before It Starts, Becoming Soul Mates, The Love List, Relationships,* and *When Bad Things Happen to Good Marriages.* They have been featured on *Oprah, CBS This Morning, CNN,* and *The View,* and in *USA Today* and the *New York Times.* They are also frequent guest speakers and have written for a variety of magazines. The Parrotts' radio program, *Love Talk,* can be heard on stations throughout North America. They live in Seattle, Washington, with their two sons.

Bring Les and Leslie to your community! Each year, the Parrotts speak to thousands of people in a variety of settings. They are entertaining, thought-provoking and immeasurably practical. One minute you'll be laughing and the next you'll sit still in silence as they open your eyes to how you can make your relationships all you want them to be.

To learn more about booking Drs. Les & Leslie Parrott for a seminar, go to www.RealRelationships.com

We want to hear from you. Please send your comments about this book to us in care of zreview@zondervan.com. Thank you.

ZONDERVAN®